Letters

TO MY

Children

by

JULIA STEWART MELTON

Unless otherwise noted, Scripture quotations are taken from the KING JAMES VERSION (*KJV*) of the Holy Bible. Amplified quotations are indicated as (*AMP*). New Living Translation quotations are indicated as (*NLT*). All versions used by permission of the copyright owners.

Published in Los Angeles, California by:
Carsamonte Glover
P.O. Box 271
Hawthorne, CA 90251
Email: CarsamontePublishing@gmail.com
In conjunction with *Carsamonte Publishing*
(CarsamontePublishing@gmail.com)

First-line and developmental editing: Carsamonte
Cover and interior Design by: DesignedByEvelyn.com
Letters to My Children was printed in the United States of America.

ISBN: 978-0-9830614-9-6

Letters TO MY *Children*

is loosely based on a true story.
The names have been changed
to protect the innocent … and the guilty.
Any similarities are coincidental.

TABLE OF
Contents

DEDICATION

This book is dedicated to every woman who has lived with the guilt and shame of abortion. I encourage you to ask God for His forgiveness and forgive yourself. God loves you with an everlasting love, from which you can never be separated. "For I am persuaded that neither death, nor life, nor angels, nor principalities, nor powers, nor things present, nor things to come. Nor height, nor depth, nor any other creature, shall be able to separate us from the love of God which is in Christ Jesus our Lord" (Romans 8:38-39). Receive His love and be free, my sister.

*"As far as the east is from the west,
so far hath he removed our transgressions from us."*
(PSALM 103:12)

ACKNOWLEDGEMENTS

First and foremost, I want to thank God for His love and for giving me the vision for this book. He has empowered me for great success!

———∾∾———

To my mother, the late Fannie Andrew-Staples. Thank you for being a woman of faith. It took some time, but I eventually followed in your footsteps. You are so beautiful to me, and I love you dearly. RIP, Mommy.

———∾∾———

To my children, Jayson, Julian, and Jared. I thank God for you. The Bible says, "Lo, children are an heritage of the Lord and the fruit of the womb is his reward. (Psalm 127:3) You have certainly been a blessing to me. You are the joy of my life. Thank you for your unconditional love and for giving purpose to my life.

———∾∾———

To my editing team, Lisa Beasley, Brenda Tate, and Carmen Glover, thanks for smoothing out the rough edges and placing the finishing touches on these pages. You are the best! I love you.

INTRODUCTION

My name is Joy Swanson, and this is my story. I guess the best place to begin is at the beginning. I was born Joy Drayton, the third child of Hattie and Robert Drayton. I entered the world at Beth Israel Hospital in Newark, New Jersey, on the 8th day of December in 1949. I was four weeks premature—a Christmas gift no one was expecting. I guess I wanted to arrive in time to get in on the holiday fun. My brother, Jake, was four years old, and my sister, Lillie, was eighteen, married, and had already had her first child by the time I arrived on the scene.

Having been born prematurely, I was very tiny. My parents used to carry me around on a pillow. Because of my peanut size, I was branded—you guessed it—Peanut. That was my nickname for the first four or five months of my life.

However, that all changed one night when a rat decided to crawl into my crib and bite me on the side of my face. I was rushed to the hospital and given medication to keep me from contracting some awful rat disease. Soon after that incident, I began to pick up weight and eventually outgrew the pillow. I had progressed to the size of a kitten, so my new nickname became Kitten.

I continued to thrive, and by the time I was a toddler I discovered my first love—my daddy. I loved my daddy! Most of my memories of him are blurred now because he was only in my life for five short years. The thing I remember so strongly is the love we shared. I always felt peaceful, safe, connected, and accepted with him. He never raised his voice or his hand at me.

I have other fond memories of walks in the park, drives in his car, and trips to a statue of Abraham Lincoln on Springfield Avenue. The statue depicts Lincoln in a sitting position, which allows space where a small child can actually sit on his lap. I would sit on Abe's lap, and daddy and I would talk and play. Then, on the way back home, he would buy me peanuts from the peanut man on High Street.

We spent a lot of time together, just the two of us, because my brother was a mama's boy. She could not go anywhere without him.

Daddy loved baseball. His team was the Brooklyn Dodgers. I was content to sit and watch the game on television with him. Now, that's love! My world was complete whenever I was with my father. There was no one I felt more connected to in my family—not even my mother.

However, one day my world crumbled in an instant when Daddy suddenly died of a heart attack. The one person I felt most connected to was gone. I was devastated and too young to express the depth of my pain. What does a five-year-old know about grief? Most adults are inept at handling grief. A young child cannot begin to fathom how to cope with such a loss. Since I had no coping mechanism in place, I grieved for my father my entire childhood. His absence affected my self-esteem and overall sense of well-being. There was a void in my heart that no one could fill. My mother tried, but I refused to let her in.

My mom remained a single parent while she raised my brother and me. It wasn't easy in those days to take care of two children on the salary of a domestic. But she was a God-fearing woman who trusted God to always provide for her family. And He did. She instilled her faith in my brother and me by making sure we attended church regularly. We spent a lot of time in church. But it kept us out of trouble and gave us a strong sense of right and wrong.

We didn't have much when it came to material things, but mom always kept a roof over our heads and food on the table. I remember being in grammar school and having only three dresses. Girls actually wore dresses to school back then. The dress I wore on Monday was the same dress I wore on Wednesday; the dress I wore on Tuesday I wore again on Thursday. The third dress was reserved for Fridays—Assembly Day. This seemed to be a good system until fifth grade. One day one of my more privileged classmates made it a point to comment on the dress I had on that day, stating that I had just worn the dress two days before. From that point, the pressure was on. I wasn't about to be caught dead wearing the same dress twice in one week. My mother had to figure out a way to get more dresses for me. And she did! She discovered the Salvation Army; it became my salvation army at the time. But it didn't last very long.

I had no clue what the Salvation Army was. One day while sporting a new dress and bragging about the fact that my mother had purchased it at the Salvation Army, a more enlightened classmate felt it was her duty to inform me that the Salvation Army was a store where poor people shopped for clothes (so much for the Salvation Army!). Once again, the pressure was on, and, once again, my ever-so-resourceful Mom came through. She began bringing home the hand-me-down clothes that belonged to the daughters of her white employers. They were nice clothes, and I kept my mouth shut about where they came from.

For the most part, I had a good childhood, but the void inside me created by my father's death continued to be a source of discontentment, which caused me to become withdrawn and detached. I had a continuous yearning for the love and acceptance that only a father can give, and I am convinced that this yearning triggered the sexual abuse I experienced as a young girl. While seeking affection, I reached out to the wrong men, and they responded to me with sex. The men who claimed to love me took advantage of me. I have since had to come to terms with the fact that I lost my virginity to a family member! The person who should have loved and protected me committed the ultimate betrayal by stealing my innocence.

And in concert with a well-scripted movie, I discovered boys, or should I say they discovered me! I am sure that's when my search to find someone to *love me* the way Daddy loved me began. That search took me on a lifelong journey filled with disappointments, pain, and unfulfilled relationships.

Over the course of my life, I have made bad choices. Specifically, on three separate occasions, I sacrificed the lives of defenseless babies because I didn't want to be woman enough or mature enough to face the certain consequences that would come as a result of my actions. Each time, I convinced myself I was making the right decision. However, these decisions proved to be the most devastating experiences of my life.

During the '70s and the '80s, abortion seemed to be the answer to unwanted or inconvenient pregnancies. I foolishly followed the trend. However, I had no idea about the effect my decisions would have on my life. Neither did I know how much pain and guilt I would feel for many years, or how I would feel about my unborn children every year around the time they would have been born.

As an insecure and frightened woman, I never considered whether I could live with my decision. I thought (or was convinced by the father of the babies) that having an abortion was the best thing to do under my circumstances during that time. What I failed to realize was that circumstances change, but once you take a life, that life is gone forever.

I had no idea how my babies would be aborted. Never did I imagine they would be ripped apart. The clinicians told me I wouldn't feel any pain. But no one told me how horrible it would be for my babies. Years later, I read about the abortion procedure I experienced, and I was appalled. It is called the suction curettage, which is the most common procedure for women between six and fourteen weeks pregnant. For those of you who may not have a clue about what the suction curettage procedure is, let me enlighten you.

> The physician must first stretch open the cervix using metal rods. Since that may be painful, he or she gives the patient a local or general anesthesia. Once the cervix is opened, the physician inserts

a hard plastic tube into the uterus. The other end of the tube is connected to a suction machine, much like the suction on a vacuum. The suction pulls the fetus' body apart and out of the uterus. Finally, the physician uses a loop-shaped knife, called a curette, to scrape the fetus and fetal parts out of the uterus. End of procedure.

I now view an abortion as a very selfish act. There is no consideration given to the unborn child's right to live. So why did I do it? I was weak, a coward. I justified my actions by thinking that extenuating circumstances warranted my decisions.

It has taken years, but the pain and guilt has decreased, especially once I repented for my actions. It was comforting to learn that I could go to God and ask His forgiveness and receive it. First John 9, in The *Amplified Bible* says:

> *"If we [freely] admit that we have sinned and confess our sins, He is faithful and just (true to His own nature and promises) and will forgive our sins (dismiss our lawlessness) and [continuously] cleanse us from all unrighteousness [everything not in conformity to His will in purpose, thought and action]."*

The revelation that God could forgive me was not only liberating; it set me on the path of self-forgiveness and healing. I finally began to accept and take responsibility for my part in the chaos and craziness going on in my life when I became pregnant with my babies. Although it's taken years, I have finally come to terms with what I've done. Today, I can honestly say I just didn't know any better. If I had known better, I most certainly would have done better.

I decided to write letters to share with the world my heart and love for those precious babies I never had the pleasure of holding in my arms. Hopefully, my story will inspire women to make better choices. Additionally, I believe these letters will finally bring closure to this very painful part of my past. Most importantly, I write these letters as a way of seeking my unborn children's forgiveness for denying them the right to live. For that, I am deeply sorry.

To women who have also made these choices, I pray you find relief for any pain and guilt you may feel when you think of your precious baby that you never had the opportunity to hold or kiss. Let me be perfectly clear; I am not addressing women who use abortion as a form of birth control. That's another book. I am speaking to those who—because of fear, lack of knowledge, or intimidation—foolishly thought abortion was the only way out of their predicament.

For those of you who have never had an abortion, I pray my story will inspire you to think long and hard before making such a decision. It is a life-altering choice that has the potential to make you a very unhappy, guilt-ridden woman, where the process of total healing will most certainly need to take place.

Dear JANUARY *Baby*

FIRST LETTER:
It's All about Control

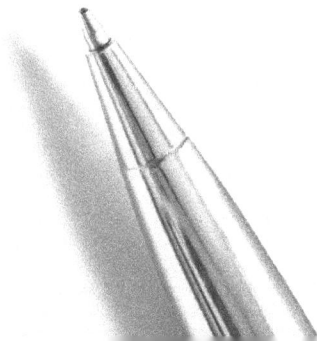

Dear January Baby,

Hi, baby. It's your mother. Someone told me babies who die before birth growup in heaven with Jesus. If that's true, I know you are having a wonderful existence in the presence of the Lord. I also heard a preacher say once that, when we die and go to heaven, we will see the babies we aborted or miscarried. I really hope that is true because I *really* want to see you!

In 1967, I got pregnant and had a miscarriage. The doctor couldn't explain why I lost the baby. He called it "an act of nature." I was seventeen years old at the time, and I really wanted the baby.

Two years later, in 1969, I met your daddy, Donald Thompson. I was nineteen, and Donald was twenty-nine. He was born and raised in North Carolina and was the second of three children born to Willie and Margaret Thompson. Donald's father owned a construction company in Newark, and I had recently been hired as his secretary. Three weeks into my employment, Mr. Thompson informed me that his two sons were going to occupy the two vacant offices.

Donald (your father) and his brother Mark were the owners of a beauty school located in Brooklyn, New York. They moved into our offices the following week, with their secretary, Marsha Williams.

Upon meeting the Thompson brothers, I thought Mark was more handsome than Donald. However, Mark was married to Kathy, and they had a son named Robert. Donald wasn't bad looking. He had nice eyes that seemed to sparkle when he smiled. I loved his eyes and his smile. He was very dark (my sister would jokingly say Donald was blue-black). Your father was about 5 foot 10, and physically fit. He had a great personality and sense of humor. He was a thinker and very analytical. I enjoyed being around him, listening to him talk and analyze things. Donald had the ability to make me talk about my feelings, something I wasn't used to doing. This once shy, introverted girl later evolved into an outgoing somewhat self-assured woman by the time I ended my relationship with your father.

Meeting Donald wasn't love at first sight, but I thought he was the most intelligent man I had ever known. He was the first man I dated who had a college degree. He could discuss anything and had an opinion about everything.

Unlike your father, I dropped out of high school at the age of 16 to earn a living. I was shy and withdrawn, and I suffered from severe low self-esteem. The only thing I had going for me was a pretty face with deep dimples and a great- looking body, which was all I needed to gain the interest of your dad.

Not long after Donald and I met, we began dating. Unfortunately, it wasn't before he had taken his secretary, Marsha, to bed a few times. I didn't know that right away. I quickly discovered this after I noticed I was dealing more with her attitude than with her! Prior to my dating your dad, Marsha and I were very friendly. She would pick me up at the bus stop on her way to work every morning. Needless to say, all of that changed when she learned I was seeing your father.

Large and in Charge

Donald lived in Elizabeth, New Jersey. He had a really nice one-bedroom apartment in a well-kept garden apartment building, with no roaches. I was impressed because all my life I had lived in low-income neighborhoods in apartments that were infested with roaches, and I hated roaches! The only thing that bothered me was the fact that he didn't own a television. Donald thought television was a waste of time. Being the intellectual he was, he chose to spend his time reading, listening to music, or simply engaging in good conversation when he wasn't being sexually active. It took some convincing, but I eventually talked him into buying a T.V.

In the beginning, I loved conversing with Donald. Sometimes we would talk all night long. We talked about everything. He was articulate, and I loved his vocabulary. I had to look up many of the words he used to learn their meaning. Between Donald and the soap operas, my vocabulary went to a new level. He really helped me sort things out about my past and set goals for my future. I often tell people he was the therapist I desperately needed during that time of my life.

I had been through so many hurtful and disappointing experiences by the time I met your dad, and he was able to talk me through those things and help me bring closure to them. He was the first person I confided in about the sexual abuse I experienced as a child at the hands of my mother's boyfriends and some of my male family members. He was so easy to talk to. Many times our sessions ended with me in tears, but a purging was taking place that was long overdue. He helped me heal emotionally and psychologically.

Donald and I began living together in the summer of 1970. We said, at the time, we were in love, but looking back, I know neither of us really knew the true meaning of love. We were in lust. Donald had a huge sexual appetite, and I had a need to leave the depressing environment I called home. Finally, I was going to live in a nice apartment with a man who didn't need me to help pay the bills, someone who was teaching me how to deal with the demons of my past. I believed I had everything to gain and nothing to lose. I later discovered how wrong I really was.

Donald was practical to a fault, and very controlling. His decisions were always based on what *he* considered practical. For instance, he didn't think it was practical for us to go out to dinner. "Why should we go out to eat when there's food at home? That's not practical," he'd say. It didn't matter that perhaps I just wanted a change of scenery or that I wanted to be in the company of others. No! Everything we needed to enjoy ourselves was right there in our apartment—food, music, books, television and, of course, each other. If we wanted to be around other people, his answer was to invite them over, or we could go to their house. It wasn't like we didn't have the money. He was just being practical and controlling. Unfortunately, I didn't realize how controlling Donald was until much later in our relationship.

Donald's parents lived in Newark, and we would visit them often. His mother was a very attractive, stylish woman with a warm personality. I liked her from the moment I met her. Mr. Thompson was my boss at the time, and at first, it was a little strange seeing him at home with his family. He was a quiet, withdrawn man at the office and at home. Your grandfather wasn't a man of many words. But, when he did speak, everyone listened. He had a commanding tone to his deep voice. From the outside looking in, it appeared that Mr. and Mrs. Thompson reared their children in a stable home environment. Donald never talked much about his childhood, so in retrospect, I wonder if there were some family skeletons he didn't want to rattle. On the other hand, Mark seemed well-adjusted in his marriage and enjoyed being a father. But who's to say what really went on behind their closed doors.

───────

Donald drove a 1969 Red Plymouth Roadrunner. It was hot! I loved that car. It was one of the popular fast cars out during that time. Drag racing was big then, and the Roadrunner, GTO, Challenger, and, of course, the sleek and sexy Corvette were very popular cars.

Many of them came with a four-speed stick shift, a hemi engine, and a four-barrel carburetor. These cars had a whole lot of power and could go from zero to sixty mph in a matter of seconds.

I had gotten my driver's license prior to meeting your dad, but I didn't know how to drive a standard, or more commonly called stick shift, automobile. Still, I really wanted to get behind the wheel of the Roadrunner. I liked the thunderous sound of the engine when it was revving, the speed, and that cute horn that sounded like the Road Runner in the Looney Tunes cartoons— beep-beep! Donald was an excellent driver, and he handled that car like a pro. Many times, when guys challenged him, he'd smoke them; I mean he'd leave them in the dust! We would have a good laugh about it. I found it all so exciting! I told him how much I wanted to learn to drive his car, and he agreed to teach me. He was a very systematic teacher.

Since I already knew how to drive, Donald decided the first thing I needed to know was where the gears were and how to shift them. So, before I was allowed behind the wheel, he thought it would be best for me to get familiar with shifting the gears. He explained the 'H' on the gear stick and what the numbers meant. After that, I began changing gears for him while he was driving. He would drive and operate the clutch while I shifted the car into the appropriate gear. After I mastered using the gear stick, he put me behind the wheel to learn how to use the clutch. That's when the fun began.

Donald would take me to a vacant parking lot behind a factory building in Rahway, New Jersey, on the weekends. It was a huge parking lot, so I had plenty of room to drive and change all four gears. After a few of these lessons, he began letting me drive back to the apartment. I must admit he was a great teacher. By the time he put me in traffic, I was handling the car perfectly.

The last thing I had to learn was how to pull off in first gear on a hill. Getting caught at a traffic light on a hill is a scary thing for someone just learning how to drive a standard automobile. The car starts to roll backward when you let up off the clutch. You must give it just the right amount of gas to make it go forward before rolling into the car or people behind you. However, if you give it too much gas, you stall out. Talk about sweating bullets! Yes, I stalled out a few times until I finally found my rhythm between the clutch and gas. It wasn't long before taking a hill became a piece of cake. Once I passed the "Donald test," he was very generous about allowing me to drive his car alone.

I can still remember how impressed my brother was that I could handle a car like that. He was so proud of me. You didn't see many women driving those hot cars back then. I was definitely hanging out with the big boys when I drove your dad's car. When men would pull up next to me at a traffic light in one of the hot cars, they would rev their engines and ask me if I wanted to run it. I'd rev my engine too, then smile and say, "You got it." Donald absolutely forbade me to race in his car, which was okay with me.

Racing was dangerous, and I was not about to put my life on the line to impress anyone.

During the fall of 1970, Donald and Mark sold their beauty school, and Donald began working at the post office in Elizabeth. So, we were no longer working in the same office. However, Mark and Marsha were still there because Mark was involved in other business ventures, and he needed Marsha's assistance.

I was glad Donald was no longer there everyday, because Marsha still wanted a relationship with him and was constantly trying to get back in his bed, even though he made it clear to her that he and I were a couple.

Some days, Donald would have me drop him off at the post office and keep the car for the day. On the days I would show up at work with Donald's car, Marsha would get an attitude and be exceptionally nasty to me. This went on for a while, and one day the two of us almost came to blows in the office.

One particular day, Marsha decided to verbally express her objection to me seeing Donald. She felt that I had taken him from her. I tried to explain to her that, according to Donald, they were not a couple; they were just friends. That seemed to make her angrier, so I thought I would really give her something to be angry about. I said, "How could I take something from you that was never yours in the first place?" By this time, we were standing in the doorway of the copy room. As I was about to exit, Marsha planted herself in front of the door in an attempt to stop me from leaving. That made me angry, and I told her that she had two seconds to move out of my way or I was going to move her! She didn't move, so I began walking through the door as if she wasn't standing there.

"Don't walk away from me b----!" she yelled. However, I kept walking, and she put her hand on my arm to turn me around. What did she do that for? I swung around and said, "Don't you ever touch me! I will f--- you up, girl!" She got the message, because she walked away and left me alone. Your mama didn't play, baby.

No Mercy

That's enough about Ms. Marsha. Let's get back to your daddy and me. As I mentioned before, Donald was generous with his car. However, he was a stickler when it came to me returning home on time. I remember taking the car one Sunday evening to visit my mother. Donald told me to be back by nine o'clock. I arrived at our apartment at ten minutes after nine. He had a fit! When I walked in the door, he yelled, "What time did I tell you to be back!"

"At nine o'clock," I said.

"What time is it now?" he asked.

I said, "It's only 9:10."

"Well, 9:10 is not nine o'clock! If you can't be back when I tell you to, don't take my car," he replied.

Mind you, it wasn't like he was planning to go anywhere. It was just another way to control me.

Another thing I found out about Donald after moving in with him was that he was an atheist. Your father didn't believe in God. I, on the other hand, believe in God and His Son, Jesus. I am a Christian. No matter how much I tried to talk to Donald about God, Jesus, or the Bible, he wanted no part of it. His excuse for being an atheist was that the Bible says Adam and Eve were the first humans on earth. His question was "if that's true, then where did the other people come from, since Adam and Eve only had two sons?" That led him to believe there was incest going on in the Garden of Eden. The pitiful part is he never read past Genesis, yet he concluded that God wasn't real and that he didn't need Him in his life. Because I was a Believer, I should never have gotten involved with him in the first place. We were truly unequally yoked in more ways than one.

A little over a year into our relationship, I told Donald I wanted to have a baby. We had already talked about marriage, and that was out. Donald had been married and divorced, and he wasn't interested in marriage at all. Although he didn't have a child with his former wife, he was as opposed to us having a baby as he was to marriage.

I told him about the miscarriage I had had two years earlier, and how much I really wanted the baby. I shared with him my relationship with the baby's father, James, who was my first love. When I was through talking, he looked very somber and asked, "You really loved him, didn't you?"

"Yes," I answered.

"I don't like him," he said.

"Why not? You don't even know him."

"I don't like him because you will never love me the way you loved him," he snapped.

I thought he was being silly, and when I told him so, he went on to say that he didn't want me to have any contact with James. He was thoroughly aggravated, and he made it quite clear that we were never going to discuss James again. I didn't know it then, but looking back, I realize my feelings for James were out of Donald's realm of control over me, and that made him feel threatened and insecure. I have since learned that most control freaks are very insecure and selfish people.

It was during one of our lengthy conversations about having a baby that I discovered just how selfish he really was. Donald's excuse for not wanting me to have a baby was that his house wasn't child-proof, and he wasn't about to make it child-proof. For some reason, he saw children as an inconvenience that would bring disorder to his very practical and organized life. Or, he would say, "A baby will ruin your figure, and I don't want that to happen." It amazed me how Donald conveniently forgot that he was once a child!

He loved my petite figure, and he wanted it to stay that way. He even tried to control what I ate so I wouldn't gain weight. I remember having to hide sweets like chocolate donuts (which I loved) in the refrigerator. I would sneak and eat them when he wasn't home. My family thought it was ridiculous when I told them, and they were right. However, it was easier for me to sneak and eat the foods he didn't approve of than to deal with him about it.

Since your father was so adamant about us not having a baby, I was on birth control. However, I experienced some bad side effects while using the pill, so I was taken off them. I tried other birth control methods that weren't as convenient or effective as the pill. Most of the time, we were careful. But, on occasion, we took chances. Some time in March of 1972, you were conceived.

I was twenty-two years old. When I found out I was pregnant, I was elated, to say the least. Donald, on the other hand, wasn't. "I told you time and time again that we are not having a baby. We are going to find a doctor to take care of this," he said. I couldn't believe he wanted me to have an abortion. I thought once he learned I was pregnant he would give in.

By this time, Mark and his wife had a new baby—another son. When he was born, Donald and I went to see them, and as I watched Donald with his nephews, he didn't seem like a man who didn't like children. He was great with them. When I mentioned this to Donald, he said, "Those are Mark and Kathy's children. They live with them. They are their responsibility, not mine. I can enjoy them because their existence doesn't prevent me from doing what I want to do." Selfish! Just plain selfish! Unfortunately, Donald was only concerned about Donald.

———⁓⁓⁓———

True to his word, Donald found a physician in Englewood, New Jersey, who would perform the abortion. I can't remember what day of the week it was, but I'll never forget the agony I felt during the ride there. From where we lived, Englewood was about a forty-five minute drive. I cried and begged Donald to let me have my baby all the way to Englewood. My tears and pleading didn't move him in the least. He stood his ground and kept driving.

I was shocked to see so many women in the waiting area when I walked in the doctor's office. Abortion was big business. I signed in and sat there, waiting my turn while Donald waited for me in the car. That just added insult to injury. After all he was putting me through, he could have at least come in with me. I don't remember feeling frightened of the procedure or for my own safety. I just remember feeling anger and resentment toward Donald and myself—Donald for demanding that I do this terrible thing, and myself for not having the courage to stand up to him.

I was given anesthesia, and when I woke up I was in the recovery room. I immediately began crying all over again. The nurse tried to console me, but to no avail. I was finally released after an hour in recovery. I hurried and dressed and left the facility. When I walked outside, Donald was right where I left him, in the car. At first I couldn't look at him. I felt loathing for him at that moment. Noticing that I was still groggy from the anesthesia, he jumped out of the car to open the door for me. He was being so attentive and tried to make conversation once he got back in the car. "Are you okay?" he asked. I just nodded. He asked me something else, but I can't remember what it was. I said, "Can we talk later? All I want to do now is go to sleep." He understood and left me alone. It was a quiet and somber ride back to Elizabeth.

That evening, I guess Donald couldn't take the silence any longer, because he asked if I wanted to go out. I told him I didn't want to go anywhere, so he decided to go visit his brother. That was the last place I wanted to go. Seeing Kathy and her children would have torn my heart to pieces. I told Donald to go without me, and he did.

The Beginning of the End

That was the turning point in our relationship. After that day, I never quite responded to Donald in the same way. I cared for him still, but something had definitely happened to the intensity of those feelings. I even began to stand my ground on certain issues. Many times, this provoked him to strike me physically, but that just gave me more reason to infuriate him. I guess, in my own way, I was trying to make him pay for what we'd done to you.

There was no going back for us after the abortion. Although we continued to try to make it work, our relationship was doomed. We were fighting more than we were getting along, and I mean fighting! He'd hit me, and I'd hit him right back. During one of our fights, he was trying to pin me down on the bed. I felt fingers near my mouth, and I thought they were his fingers, so I bit down on them as hard as I could. To my surprise, they were my fingers! After that, I realized something had to give before someone really got hurt. I wasn't trying to be in an abusive relationship. That wasn't for me, and I thank God I had enough sense to realize that.

During this time, Donald's father and his business partner went out of business. Donald persuaded me to take some time off from working. It sounded like a good idea at the time, but when he started coming home for lunch every day and I discovered I was part of the daily menu, being at home became old *real quick*. He was wearing me out, and my out was to get another job! It wasn't long before I landed one with the State of New Jersey Division of Youth and Family Services, as a transcriptionist. The office happened to be around the corner from our apartment. It was so convenient that I could walk there and come home for lunch if I wanted to. I really loved that job. I even considered becoming a social worker, but Donald thought I'd be too emotional and bring my work home. When I think about it, he was quite negative about anything I wanted to do that didn't line up with his plans for me.

I remember how negative he was when I wanted to become a flight attendant. I applied for a job with Eastern Airlines. I went through the testing and interviews and was offered the opportunity to go to Texas for training. When I told Donald, he looked at me and said, "All I can say is call before you come home." Well, what that translated to was, since the job required me to travel, he would see other women in my absence. So, of course, I didn't go for the training. Once again I allowed Donald to control me.

Our relationship continued to deteriorate, and when Donald started asking me to "swing" with him and other couples, I knew I had to get away from him. Donald was crossing over into what translated to me as freaky, ungodly things that I wanted no part of. I asked him why he wanted us to be swingers. He said, "Variety is the spice of life, and I want variety without having to cheat on you." I couldn't believe he had no problem with another man sleeping with me. He went on to say that the *good* thing about swinging is there aren't any emotional ties. It's just sex. Everybody has a good time and then you go home with your significant other.

He was very passionate about the swinging thing—so much so that he would get violent when I would say no, or when I simply didn't want to discuss it at all. I began to wonder, *who is this man?*

Donald's relentless nagging about swinging continued until I finally decided I was going to move back home with my mother. Leaving him wasn't as hard as I thought it would be. Donald didn't protest because, by then, he had started seeing the daughter of his father's business partner. He had known her since she was a young girl. Apparently, he had been watching her with lust in his heart over the years. She was now of age for him to act on his feelings, and she was attracted to him.

Before I moved out, he had the nerve to bring her to the apartment one evening. I guess he was still trying to make a point about swinging. The point being, with him in a relationship with her, I was left out. On the other hand, if I agreed to swing with him, I'd be included. The way he saw it, either I could be a swinger with him or he'd do his own thing without me. I couldn't believe how insensitive he was to entertain another woman in the house we shared. Was there no end to his need to control? That night was the icing on the cake for me.

Not long after that awful night I moved, but I didn't move back home with my mother. Living in a nice apartment away from the ghetto made me want more for my life. By this time, I had left the Division of Youth and Family Services and was working for the Union County Courthouse, making more money than I ever had in my life. So I decided to continue living on my own. I moved into an apartment in the same town, about ten minutes from Donald. I was twenty-three years old and ready to live my own life.

On My Own

After I moved out of your father's apartment, I had a lot of time to think about our relationship. I was very bitter toward him and held a lot of unforgiveness in my heart. I needed to bring closure to all the hurt and disappointment I experienced with him. Donald taught me how to analyze and think things through, so it wasn't long before I would come to grips with the negative things that happened between us. I was also able to see my fault in the demise of our relationship. And what I saw wasn't very pretty.

My darling January baby, your mama was weak, immature, and insecure. As badly as I wanted you, I should never have allowed anyone to talk me into having an abortion. My first mistake was not telling my family. Donald told me not to tell anyone about the pregnancy. Of course, in an effort to please him, I did what he said. However, had I told my family, they would have given me as many reasons to keep you as your father did to abort you. My family didn't condone abortion. They believed that you have your children and do the best you can for them. I know now they would have supported me and given me the courage to have you despite Donald's disapproval. I came from a Christian family, and I knew better. However, I did not set boundaries, so it was easy to be influenced by others. That's what happened. I allowed Donald to enforce his beliefs and morals on me. I stopped going to church and reading the Bible while I was with him, and it really cost me a lot where my relationship with God was concerned. God wasn't able to lead and guide me in the way I should go, because I stopped listening for and to His voice. That was the worst mistake of all. Like Donald, I took God out of the equation, and my life ended up a mess without Him in it.

All of this happened over forty years ago. Please know that a year hasn't gone by without me thinking of you, especially during the month of January. I hope this letter explains why I did what I did. I pray that you understand and will forgive me. I don't know how life would have been had you lived, but I do know that I would have done my best to be a good mother and role model for you.

I've seen Donald a few times over the years, and he has not changed his mind about marriage or having children. To my knowledge, he still does not have a family. I kept in touch with his mother for a while after our breakup. Years later, I ran into her and Mr. Thompson at a church function. I was happy to see that he had given his life to the Lord and was working in the church. He was still very quiet and withdrawn, but he seemed happy. Of course I asked Mrs. Thompson about Donald, and she said he was doing well and was still single. *How sad*, I thought. Family is the most important thing a person can have. I'm glad I moved on and experienced the blessings and joy of having a family of my own.

About two years after Donald and I broke up, I met a man named Rodney. He and I became lovers, and we had two sons together. Because of my experience with Donald, I had the courage to stand up to Rodney. I made it clear from the very beginning that I would not have an abortion if I became pregnant. It simply was not an option.

The birth of your brothers didn't ease the pain of aborting you; neither did it dissolve the regret. I will always regret not having you. You have a special place in my heart that no one can ever occupy. I look forward to the day when we meet in heaven. Yes, I am determined to get there. You and three of your siblings are there now, and I want to see all of you.

January baby, I love you, and I'll continue to think of you always until the day we are finally together.

Your loving mother,

Joy

Quiet Moments: Write Your Own Letter

Dear MAY *Baby*

SECOND LETTER:
Everything Good to You Isn't Good for You

Dear May Baby,

Wow, where do I begin? There was so much going on in my life when you were conceived. It was 1978, and I was single with two sons. Their father and I had recently ended a four-year relationship, and, to say the least, the thought of raising two children alone was frightening. I was lonely, which is why it was easy for me to, once again, fall into the arms of your father.

Your father's name is Michael Harris, and he was twenty-nine at the time. He was the lead singer of a local gospel group. What a dynamic and energetic performer! Not only did he have great vocal skills, but he also knew how to captivate his audience. He commanded the stage from the moment he stepped on it. It was easy to forget all about the other three men on stage with him. He was the kind of entertainer that made the audience exhausted just from watching his over-the-top performance.

Michael was handsome, funny, and smart. He stood about 5 foot 10 and was the color of dark chocolate. He was extremely charming.

I'll never forget our first meeting. It was 1965, and we were still in high school. I was fifteen years old and a sophomore, and Michael was seventeen and a senior. My best friend, Lisa, was also fifteen. One Friday night my mother took us to church, and Michael and his singing group were there. They were dressed alike, in black slacks and white shirts. When they got up to sing, I could not take my eyes off Michael! Lisa, on the other hand, was quite taken with the guitar player, who we later learned was Michael's brother. After the group finished singing, they went out of the sanctuary into the lobby of the church. Lisa and I followed. We told my mother we were going to the restroom, but our real mission was to introduce ourselves to those good-looking brothers. I must admit we were impressed to see guys our age in church singing for the Lord.

Lisa and I struck up a conversation with the two brothers, and as it turned out, they had their eyes on us as well. I noticed while talking to Michael that he awakened feelings in me I didn't know existed. The attraction was immediate and very physical. Before leaving church that night, we exchanged phone numbers.

Michael and I talked on the phone every day after school for weeks before we saw each other again. One evening I managed to get out of the house to see Michael. He picked me up and took me to his cousin's house. His cousin was married, and his wife worked nights. In his wife's absence, his cousin allowed Michael to entertain his girlfriends there. Michael and I went into one of the bedrooms, and there we made love for the first time. It was like nothing I had ever experienced in my life! I experienced my first orgasm, and a soul tie began that would last for decades.

From that first time many years ago, until in my forties, I had the hardest time resisting Michael's sexual advances. No matter how many times I would say "no," my body seemed to always yell "YES!" He had charisma, and I was drawn to him. I remember trying to convince Michael, after I became born-again "for real," that we couldn't sleep together because it was wrong in the eyes of God. Well, don't you know he found a way to get around that? He went so far as to quote scripture to convince me that the two of us committing fornication wasn't a big thing. He quoted the scripture that says, "For all have sinned and come short of the glory of God." Being a babe in Christ at that time, and unable to rightly divide the Word, I foolishly listened to him rather than what I believed to be true in my heart.

I knew he wasn't right for me. Back in the day, Michael was what we called a *ladies man*. He loved the ladies! But I felt I had to have him. There were times during our relationship that I would deliberately avoid him because I knew I was just his "good time" girl, and I wanted to be so much more. But no matter how hard I tried to resist him, I would fail. He had a way of sweet- talking me right out of my underwear.

My Big Mistake

Michael had been married twice. Ironically, we never hooked up when he was between wives. Other than in high school, all of our sexual rendezvous took place while he was married to one of his wives. I often wonder what would have happened had we really tried being a couple rather than mere sex buddies. Would we have experienced the same passion and chemistry? We may never know.

That was the situation in the summer of 1978; we somehow found our way back into each other's arms. We hadn't been in touch for years. I was with Rodney, your brothers' father, and pretty much out of the loop of things, especially where church was concerned. Rodney wasn't into church, and I didn't go too much while I was with him. However, by the end of our relationship, I had joined a church and had begun singing in the choir. I think that was the straw that broke the camel's back for Rodney and me.

Strange as it may seem, from the very beginning, church was always where Michael and I would run into each other. It was never in traffic, at a store, in the mall, or at someone's house. Church was our meeting ground. One Sunday in August, my choir was invited to sing at a choir anniversary at a local church. To my surprise, Michael and his group were on the program. My knees almost buckled when I saw him standing in the lobby looking like a model straight out of *GQ* magazine, all dressed up in a white suit. He walked over to me with his sexy smile, hugged me, and said, "Hey, good looking!"

"Hi, Michael," I said, smiling all over myself.

"I haven't seen you in years! Where you been hiding?" he asked.

"I've been around," I said.

"I want your phone number before you leave, okay?" he asked.

"We'll see," I replied, knowing all the while that I was going to give that fine man my phone number.

A few nights later, Michael called and asked if he could come over. I had just gotten home from choir rehearsal and was in the process of getting my sons ready for bed. I was tired and feeling a little overwhelmed, and I thought it would be nice to have some adult company. Although I knew it was his typical *booty call*, I said yes. Once again, I couldn't resist being with him.

When he arrived, my boys were still up finishing a light snack before going to bed. Michael could tell I was a bit frazzled, so he suggested that I go and relax in the tub for a few moments. He offered to keep the boys occupied. I thought that was sweet of him, and I took him up on his offer. While I sat in the tub, I could feel the tension leaving my body. I became so comfortable I nearly fell asleep. After my bath, I returned to the living room where Michael and your brothers were romping around having a good time. After they went to bed, so did we. That was the night you were conceived.

The sad part about that night was that I had birth control that I could have used, but I didn't. I was lost in the moment, and I didn't have enough sense to protect myself. It was a reckless act with serious consequences. I should have known better. And I paid for it dearly.

When your father was about to leave that night, we stood at the door in each other's arms. We'd kiss goodnight, and he'd start to walk out. Then he'd turn back and kiss me again. We went back and forth like that several times. Finally, he whispered, "I can't get enough of you, Joy."

"Same here," I breathlessly replied.

The passion between us was intoxicating. We kissed one last time. When he stepped on the other side of the door, I said, "Get home safely" and quickly closed the door. Four weeks later, I learned you were growing inside me.

I was devastated. If I could have, I would have kicked my own self in the butt! I remember crying all the way home from the doctor's office. I hadn't heard from Michael since the night of your conception, and I had no way of reaching him to tell him I was pregnant. I felt foolish, used, and frightened. *How in the world was I going to care for three children alone,* was the question I kept asking myself. Your brothers were four and two—babies! I was so ashamed of myself, and the fact that I hadn't heard from Michael didn't help.

The nurse at the doctor's office had given me a card with the name of a local clinic that performed abortions. During that time, abortions were so prevalent among single women that clinicians routinely asked women if they wanted to have the baby. If she said no, they would refer her to a doctor or clinic. Frightened and distraught at the thought of being pregnant and unable to contact Michael, I thought my only choice was to abort you.

You see, baby, I had finally found peace and joy in my life. I lived in a nice apartment with your two brothers; I had a good job, and belonged to a church where I was growing spiritually. At the time, I saw you as an intrusion. I could not have you because your birth would have revealed my dirty little secret—that I was a foolish woman trying to make it in society, not the strong, mature mother of two small children I was desperately trying to portray. Not to mention the fact that I had no idea when or if I would ever see Michael again. Even if he knew, what could he do to help me? After all, he was a married man with two children of his own. I had to fix this situation on my own, and that is what I did.

In October 1978, I went and had you, my embarrassing secret, taken care of. Once again, I sat alone, waiting my turn to have you ripped from my womb. I was too embarrassed and ashamed to tell anyone I was pregnant. I was professing to be a Christian, yet I willingly slept with a married man without using birth control. As a result, I was about to take the life of an innocent child. I felt like the lowest of the low.

I returned home defeated and overwhelmed by the thought of killing another child. I think the worse part about *this* abortion was having to deal with knowing that I could have prevented the pregnancy by abstaining from sexual sin. I was so careless and so disappointed in myself. This was just another example of my inability to take responsibility for my actions. I couldn't face the possibility of having another child out of wedlock, especially by a man who was married to another woman. What would I tell my family? The more I thought about it, the more I hated myself for being careless and cowardice.

After the abortion, I vowed never to be intimate with Michael again. I wanted to change and become the kind of woman who could be proud of the choices she makes. I had two children depending on me to be wise and not foolish. I rededicated my life to Christ and threw myself into my children and church. I didn't date and didn't want to. I needed to learn how to say no and mean it.

One month later, Michael resurfaced. One night, while lying in bed trying to go to sleep, the telephone rang. Guess who? It was Michael. After we went through the customary pleasantries, he made his move.

"You feel like a little company?" he asked.

"No, I don't," I answered. "As a matter of fact, I have something to tell you," I continued.

I told Michael about the pregnancy and the abortion. I told him how miserable the whole ordeal had been for me and that I resented the fact that I couldn't get in touch with him. He listened attentively and was somewhat speechless when I was done. He asked, "When did you have the abortion?"

"Last month."

More silence.

I asked him why he was so quiet.

"Last month I had an accident and wrecked my car," he answered.

He said he believed the accident was his punishment for his role in the decision I was forced to make. Maybe it was. I don't know.

Michael understood all too well why I didn't want to see him that night, and for the first time since I'd known him, he didn't persist. I could tell he felt remorse over what had happened. When we hung up, I knew I wouldn't hear from him again. And, for a long time, I didn't.

I moved on with my life and tried to forget what I had done. Months later, I finally told two of my friends about the abortion. My girlfriend Stacy tried to make me feel better by saying that I shouldn't beat myself up. She said the last thing I needed was another mouth to feed. She also wished I had told her so she could have gone with me. "No one should have to go through that alone," she said.

My oldest and dearest friend, Lisa, on the other hand, was happy I didn't have Michael's baby. In her book, he was a male whore who didn't mean me or any other woman any good. Her dislike for Michael made her insensitive to what I had done to you. When I explained to her how badly I felt about destroying a life, she said I shouldn't place all the blame on myself—that Michael left me no other choice, especially since he was nowhere to be found.

"Lisa, I often wonder if my baby was a little girl," I said.

"Girl, I doubt that. Michael can't make a precious little girl. It was a knuckle-headed boy," she teased.

A knuckle-headed boy or not, you were my child, and I never should have denied you the right to live. Yes, things would have probably been rough. And I would have had to face the embarrassment of another out-of-wedlock pregnancy in front of my family and church. But I know now that God would have made a way for me, and my family and church would have supported me during that difficult time. However, once again, I didn't have the courage to take responsibility for my actions, and I didn't have enough faith in God and the people who loved me to do what was right.

That was a long time ago, and I haven't forgotten about you in all these years. Every May I pause and think about the child that would have been born in spring. I feel I owe you so much because I made bad decisions that cost you your life. I would do anything to make it up to you.

Heaven is so dear to me because you are there. Jesus is coming soon, and I'll be coming to heaven. If He tarries and I cross over before then, that is okay too, because that means I will get there sooner. I will be the one asking for my May baby.

Your loving mother,
Joy

Quiet Moments: Write Your Own Letter

_____

_____

_____

_____

_____

_____

_____

_____

_____

_____

_____

_____

_____

_____

_____

_____

_____

_____

_____

_____

_____

Dear
DECEMBER
Baby

THIRD LETTER:
When You Play With Fire, You Will Get Burned

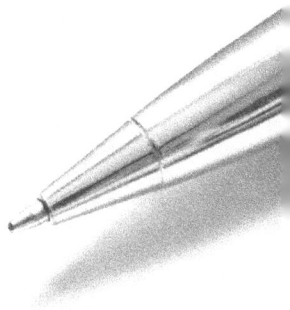

Dear December Baby,

You would think I would have learned my lesson from the last episode that resulted in me having to go through an abortion, but I didn't. Exactly five weeks later, I was on my way to making yet another bad decision. The only difference this time was that your father wasn't married. He was engaged, and his fiancé was pregnant with their child.

I met your father, Andre Walker, in the fall of 1978. I was twenty-nine, and he was twenty-four when he came into my life like a breath of fresh air. Andre and my friend Stacy attended the same church and had become friends who enjoyed a totally platonic relationship. Andre had recently moved to New Jersey to live with his father and start a new job.

One evening, Stacy and Andre stopped by my house. This was my first time meeting Andre, and I must admit I was somewhat attracted to him. He was cute with a deep, sexy voice. He was a little on the chunky side, but he looked good in his clothes. He smelled good and had a lovely smile that seemed to light up the room. I've always been a sucker for a good-looking, good-smelling man, especially one with a nice smile.

Physically, Andre stood about five-foot-nine, and his skin color; pecan brown. His lips were so inviting—the kind I wanted to kiss. His eyes were brown and very revealing. His emotions shined brightly through his eyes. They were truly the windows of his soul. His eyes sometimes spoke louder than his words. Besides his physical attributes, Andre was very articulate and was a great listener as well, which I found equally stimulating.

Stacy and Andre brought marijuana with them, and we spent the evening getting high. Even though I was in the Church and trying to live right, I still had a taste for and enjoyed smoking weed. I had not yet decided to stop.

I was working for Prudential Insurance Company in downtown Newark, and during our conversation, I learned Andre worked there also. I also learned that his pregnant fiancée lived in Pennsylvania. Her name was Yvette. Andre kept us entertained that night, and by the time he and Stacy left my apartment, I felt as though I had known him forever.

When I spoke with Stacy the next day, she said, "Girl, Andre likes you and wants to see you again."

"I'd like to see him again too," I said.

"I noticed the two of you making goo-goo eyes," she teased.

"He's cute, with his chunky self," I said.

"Yeah, I knew you were attracted to him. It's that jelly butt, isn't it?" she laughed.

I admitted to Stacy that he looked good to me. We had a big laugh about his jelly butt, which became my and Stacy's nickname for Andre. I told her to give him my telephone number, and she said she would.

As fate would have it, before Andre got a chance to call me, our paths crossed at work one day. I was on my way to the company cafeteria, and there he was. He was leaving the cafeteria and heading back to work. We were happy to see each other and talked briefly. Andre said he would give me a call that night; he kept his word. We talked on the telephone for hours. He told me a lot about his life up to that point, and he talked about Yvette. He said he loved her and was excited about the baby, but he wasn't sure if he was ready to get married. He hadn't really found his niche in life. He was in the management trainee program at Prudential, beginning his climb up the corporate ladder. He had big dreams and was very determined to rise above his meager beginnings in Pennsylvania. I found his youth and ambition exciting—so much so that I totally dismissed the fact that he admitted being in love with his fiancée. Who deliberately begins a relationship with someone who's already in love with someone else? Unfortunately, I did. As we used to say back in the day, I was *cruising for a bruising*.

By the time we got off the phone that night, we knew we wanted to spend time with each other, and made plans to do so. What I didn't suspect when I began seeing Andre was that, in just a few short months, I would be in the same predicament I had just gotten out of with Michael.

Andre and I began having lunch together regularly. Before long, we started seeing each other after working hours, either at my house or his. Our evenings together usually consisted of listening to music and playing a game of backgammon while engaging in conversation, before yielding to the passion that was so strong between us. Andre was an attentive and gentle lover. He made me feel like my pleasure was most important to him, not his own. That was something very new to me, and I liked it. It wasn't long before we were spending most of our free time together, except on the weekends. Andre went to Pennsylvania on the weekends to visit his fiancée. However, from Sunday evening to Thursday, if at all possible, we were together.

No Turning Back

A month had gone by, and Christmas of '78 was approaching. Andre was planning to spend the holidays in Pennsylvania with his family and fiancée. Before leaving New Jersey, he took me out to dinner. We went to a very nice restaurant in West Orange. On the ride there, we listened to a gospel tape he had in his car. I can't remember the name of the woman singing, but she had a beautiful voice, and the songs on the tape were so inspiring. I told Andre that I had to have a copy of that tape, and he promised to make one for me. He kept his promise; Andre always kept his promises.

Both of us loved gospel music, and the ride to the restaurant was so like him— comfortable, enjoyable, and tranquil. When we arrived at the restaurant, I was quite impressed. It was one of West Orange's elite spots, with valet service and a very intimate atmosphere. During dinner, Andre expressed his *deep* feelings for me and said he was confused as to what to do about them. He admitted that, even though he had an obligation to his fiancée and their unborn child, he wanted me in his life too. He said he never knew it was possible to love two women at the same time. I confessed to him that the relationship had gone past fun and games for me and that I was falling in love with him. That night we realized we had bitten off more than we could chew. Andre left the next day for Pennsylvania, and I missed him terribly while he was away.

I really enjoyed Andre and the time we spent together. I found him intellectually stimulating. He reminded me of Donald in that way. Andre taught me how to play backgammon, which I enjoy playing to this day, and we enjoyed talking to one another. We were becoming extremely close, yet we knew our affair had to end. His fiancée's due date was rapidly approaching. The plan was that, after the baby was born birth, they would come to New Jersey to live. Our time was just about up. When Andre returned after the holidays, we tried to put the brakes on. We limited our time together, but that wasn't working. We stopped having lunch together every day. We cut back to two or three times a week. *Hey, every little bit helps,* I thought. When that didn't work, we decided to go cold turkey and stop all communication. Each time we tried to end it, we only ended up back in each other's arms for that proverbial last time. We struggled to stay in control of our emotions but failed miserably. We were too far gone. We should have stopped while we were ahead, which was probably after the first time. In fact, we never should have started at all.

Three months later, in early March of '79, Andre and I were lying in his bed watching television. Johnny Mathis and Denise Williams were guests on one of the talk shows. It may have been *The Merv Griffin Show*. I really don't remember. The duo sang their hit song, "Too Much, Too Little, Too Late." When they started singing, Andre and I looked at each other because we knew they were singing our song. Andre couldn't lie there and listen to them sing. He got up and left the room. The chorus goes like this:

Too much, too little, too late, to ever try again,
Too much, too little, too late, let's end it being friends.
Too much, too little, too late, we knew it had to end.
It over, it's over.

I sat there and cried. It was like the handwriting was on the wall. That song confirmed everything we had been feeling for the past couple of months. We had to get over each other and move on. Once again, we tried to say goodbye.

We managed to stay away from each other for about three weeks. We purposed to avoid running into each other at work. I stopped going to lunch at my usual time and stayed away from the employee lounge, which is where we would meet. Prudential was very generous to its employees. We had a great cafeteria with delicious food that was very inexpensive and an employee lounge, equipped with pool tables, televisions, and a library. It was a great place for people to meet and unwind for an hour.

The company was also famous for hosting trips during the winter and summer months. It was winter, and the company was providing a ski trip to a resort in upstate New York. A couple of my coworkers were going, and they talked me into going also. I was happy about going because it would get me out of town for a few days and away from the temptation to call Andre. I went on the ski trip during the three weeks Andre and I managed to stay away from each other. Needless to say, I had a miserable time. I thought of him day and night.

Sunday, the last day of my trip, I called Stacy and learned from her that Andre's fiancée had given birth to their son. Andre was in Pennsylvania. His father, Sam, who was also a member of Stacy's church, had given her the news earlier that day. "Stacy, I can't stop thinking about him."

"Girl, you gotta get over it. Andre is going to marry her," she said.

"I know. I thought I was just having fun with him, but I really do love him."

"He was supposed to be your good time guy, not the love of your life. Let him go, Joy."

"You're right. I'm too old to act this way. I'm going to stick to my guns and leave Andre alone," I replied.

That's what I said, but that is not what I did.

One for the Road

I really missed Andre. I missed the sound of his calming voice, his peacefulness, and even his disposition. Andre was easy like a Sunday morning. I missed him calling me *mon amour,* which is French for "my love." He was so romantic, and I loved it!

If there was a dark side to his personality, I never saw it. We never argued. On the few occasions when there was some tension between us, his solution was to talk it through and come to an amicable resolution. I loved that about him. He didn't allow me to hold stuff in. He'd pull it out of me. Andre would start by asking me ever so gently, in that deep, sexy voice, "Why are you so subdued?" After I finished melting at the sound of his voice, I'd offer a reply. We'd spend the next few hours, or however long we had together, getting rid of the negative tension and returning to that place of comfort and sensuality that never failed to overtake us.

When I returned from the ski trip, I was hell-bent on staying away from Andre. When I went to work the next day, I took every precaution not to run into Andre. I wasn't sure if he was at work, so, to play it safe, I went to lunch with a few co-workers. They were still reveling over the good time they had had at the ski resort and decided to go to one of the local restaurants for lunch. I pretended to join in the revelry and went along. The day went by slowly, and I made it through without seeing or hearing from Andre. Part of me was happy, yet another part of me was terribly sad.

That evening, when I arrived home, I went through the motions of feeding your brothers and getting them ready for bed. A little after the last dish had been washed and put away, and our clothes had been laid out for the next day, the telephone rang. I stood there for a moment, staring at the telephone, trying to decide if I should answer. About the fourth ring, I snatched the receiver and answered, "Hello."

"Hey, baby," Andre said.

"Hey," I managed to get out as I sat down on my bed.

"I just got back from Pennsylvania this evening."

So, he wasn't at work today, I thought. But I remained silent.

"I called Stacy last night to find out if you were back from the ski trip," Andre said.

I still couldn't speak.

"Did she tell you my son was born three days ago?" he asked.

Finally finding my voice, I answered, "Yes. Congratulations."

"Thank you. I wanted to tell you, but you were away."

I was silent again.

"Joy, this should be the happiest time of my life, but I'm miserable."

I said, "Andre, please. We can't …"

"I want to see you," he interrupted. "I miss you so much, mon amour."

Why in the hell did he have to go there? And why in the hell did he have to call me *mon amour*? I was losing the battle quickly, and before I knew it, I was saying, "Yes, I'll come over."

My girlfriend Michelle lived in the apartment next door. She was single and loved my little boys. She often babysat for me, and as I dashed over to her apartment, I was praying she was available to come over and sit with the boys. She was, and as soon as I changed my clothes, I was on my way to Andre's house.

When I got there, I sat in my car for a few minutes, trying to convince myself to leave and go back home. But I didn't. My only explanation for getting out of my car that night was that Andre was a breath of fresh air that gently blew into my life at a time when I desperately needed someone. He fulfilled me on many levels, and I didn't want to give him up.

I rang the bell. He opened the door, and we fell into each other's arms. It was like a scene from a movie. Every reserve and restraint we thought we possessed left us the moment we saw each other. We stood there in the doorway just holding each other—not a word was spoken. It was the most intense moment I had ever experienced. And that night, my sweet December baby, was the night you were conceived.

Andre and I continued seeing each other through March of '79. By that time, reality was staring me dead in the face, and I couldn't deal with it. His fiancée was preparing to move to New Jersey with their son the following month. As long as she was in Pennsylvania I could cope, but once girlfriend moved to New Jersey, I knew I would not be able to take it. So, for the last time, I made up my mind that it was over—that I was going to end my relationship with Andre. To my surprise, I got through my last meeting with him without backing down. It was an emotional meeting for both of us. There were tears, and we held on to each other like there was no tomorrow, but, in the end, we did what we knew we had to do—say goodbye.

April finally arrived, and, as planned, Andre's fiancée and son moved in with him. I was determined to move on and put the whole Andre experience behind me. That was easier said than done, but somehow I managed to stay strong until later that month, when I found out I was pregnant.

A little later in the month I saw a job posting for a position in the travel department at Prudential. I applied for the job, and after two successful interviews, I was hired. I was one of four travel agents responsible for making travel arrangements for managers and executives traveling on company and/or personal business. I really liked what I was doing. It was in a fast- paced office environment, and I didn't have time to reminisce over Andre. It was the best thing that had happened to me in a long time.

However, there was just one thing that wasn't so great about the new job. My office was located in the annex area of the Prudential complex, with large windows in the front. There were clothing stores and restaurants located in that area, with a walkthrough to the other Prudential building located on the other side of the annex. The traffic outside our office was heavy, with shoppers and other employees scurrying to and from the other building. Andre often passed by my office to go to his building, and he would wave to me. Seeing him pass by wasn't always a good thing for me. For the first time, we were trying to have a platonic relationship. We just wanted to be friends, if that was possible. It wasn't easy, but we were making progress.

We didn't go to lunch together anymore, but we occasionally took our breaks together or spoke on the telephone for a few minutes to keep in touch. We didn't dare see each other outside of work. One day, during a brief encounter with Andre, he showed me photos of his son. He was a cute little boy who had many of his father's features. I could see he was going to be a miniature version of Andre.

During these meetings, we tried to console each other emotionally. Somehow I managed to act as his sounding board as he tried to sort out his emotions. No one knew better than I what he was going through, and vice versa. The hardest part for me, however, was discussing his relationship with *"her."*

I could tell his guilt was really getting to him as he told me how Yvette had questioned him about his feelings. She felt something had changed between them. She said she could even see it in his eyes when he looked at her. Although he tried to convince her that everything was fine, she wasn't buying it and was beginning to feel unwanted. My theory is he couldn't convince her because he had not convinced himself.

"I feel as though I should tell her about us, but I don't want to hurt her. Yet, I sense that I'm hurting her anyway," he said. "Then

I have to consider our families. Everyone is so excited about the baby and the upcoming wedding. I talked to my Dad about this, and he said I have too much to lose, and too many people will be hurt if I back out now. He thinks I should chalk our relationship up to a big mistake and move on. That's easy for him to say."

"Your father is right," I said. "As much as I would love for you to be with me, I don't want it to be at someone else's expense. What we have now is special, but can we sustain it in the midst of the drama you'll experience if you break up with Yvette? Besides, what about your son?"

"I love my son," he said.

"Do you love her?" I asked.

"I love both of you," he answered.

"Well, you can't have both of us. Look, Andre, if you can't do what's right for you, then do what's right for your son," I managed to say.

At this point, I was beginning to get tired of the whole emotional roller coaster we were on. I realized then that there was no way out of this mess without someone getting hurt, and I certainly didn't want it to be his son.

Near the end of April, I noticed I hadn't had a period in a while. I began feeling nauseous. I took a pregnancy test, and it was positive. Damn! I thought I was going to die. It had only been six months since the last pregnancy, and here I was once again in another messed up situation. Careless, reckless behavior had once again taken me down the same stupid path.

Of course I told Stacy, and she looked at me like I had two heads. Even though she didn't say it, I know she was thinking *you stupid b----!* Stacy was a no-nonsense kind of woman. The reason we were as close as we were is because she was the kind of friend who didn't lie to you. She told it like it was. I could always count on Stacy to be straight-up with me. On the other side of that was a sensitive, kind person who didn't believe in kicking someone when she was down. Stacy knew I was devastated, and I thank God she didn't say what was really on her mind.

Like me, Stacy had two children, but they were much older than mine. Her daughter was sixteen, and her son was thirteen. After the birth of her son, she had her tubes tied. Stacy's maternal instincts began and ended with *her* children. Children were not her favorite people. So it was easy for these words to come flowing out of her mouth, "I know you're not going to have that baby."

"I cannot have another abortion, Stacy. Besides, I want my baby."

"Are you crazy! How in the hell are you going to support another child? You are already raising two children by yourself. And what about Andre? Does he know?"

"No, he doesn't know yet."

"Did you forget he's getting married in a few weeks? Do you think he's going to be around to help you with your baby?"

"No, I have not forgotten that he's getting married, and I do not know what he will or will not do where my baby is concerned Stacy," I said.

"I thought the reason you chose not to have Michael's baby was because you did not want to have another child out of wedlock. Joy, what are you thinking about?"

"I cannot keep having abortions, Stacy," I yelled.

"Then stop getting pregnant," she yelled back. "I do not understand it. You have birth control, but you don't use it. What is up with that?"

"Stacy, have you ever heard of getting caught up in the moment?" I asked.

"Have you ever heard of the pill?"

"Girl, you know I can't take birth control pills," I snapped.

"Then maybe you need to get your tubes tied, Joy."

"Maybe you need to go straight to hell, Stacy!"

I was pissed off mainly because I knew she was right. I had been careless about using my birth control. But I did not stay angry with her for long. We made up that evening, even though she remained adamant about me having an abortion, despite my wanting to have you.

When I arrived at work the next day, I called Andre and asked if he would meet me in the annex. He said he would meet me there at noon. When he arrived, I was feeling sick, and it showed. The first thing he said was, "What's wrong? You don't look well." That was the understatement of the month! No, I wasn't well, and under the circumstances, had no idea when I would be well again. We went to a local restaurant and got a table right away. After we settled in, he asked, "What's the matter?"

"I'm pregnant," I said, as the tears began to cloud my eyes.

"Call it premonition, but ever since that last night we were together, I've had a feeling that you were pregnant," he said.

"That was the night," I said. "We knew we were taking a chance. I purposely didn't bring my birth control because I was determined not to sleep with you. But I did."

"What do you want to do?" he asked.

"It's not about what I want to do. It's about what I have to do!" I snapped.

"What do you mean by that?"

"In my heart I want to have this baby, but in all practicality, I can't. You are weeks away from your wedding, and I *don't* want to have another child out of wedlock."

I could hear the sadness in his voice when he said, "I want our baby. I wish I could take care of you and your children so you can have my baby."

"I wish you could too, but you can't. We both know what I have to do," was my cold reply.

For the first time in our relationship, the feeling of anger over the entire situation was beginning to overtake me. Things were going from bad to worse, and I only wanted my peace of mind back. Andre and I had run into a brick wall. We couldn't go back, and we couldn't go forward, and I didn't like how that felt.

We continued our conversation over lunch, and I summoned up the courage to tell him how I was going to handle our *little* dilemma. I said I was going to make an appointment with my doctor to find out how far along I was in the pregnancy. Then, I was going to make arrangements for the abortion. Andre wasn't happy about it, but he knew he couldn't offer me a better solution. He did say that he would take care of any costs and that he would go with me. I appreciated that. For the remainder of our lunch, the atmosphere at our table was somber, to say the least. Andre walked me back to my office and kissed me gently before walking away. I stood there and watched him walk through the annex until he was out of sight.

Here I Go Again

I was fortunate (at least that is what I thought at the time) to get a doctor's appointment the following week. The doctor confirmed that I was six weeks pregnant. He asked if I wanted to have the baby, and I said no. Ironically, the doctor he referred me to was located in Englewood, New Jersey. I wondered if it was the same practice I had gone to for my first abortion. I couldn't be sure because I didn't remember the street address or the doctor's name. But just the thought of going to Englewood once again to have an abortion was disturbing.

I called and made the appointment for the procedure, which was scheduled for the following Saturday. I called Andre and told him when and where the appointment was. He said he'd pick me up and drive me there. I don't know how he got out of the house on a Saturday morning, but he did.

The morning of the procedure, Andre called me before he left home to ask me one more time if I'd reconsider. I told him no. "That's our baby," he said.

"Andre, please! I can't handle this pressure today. I can't have this baby. Just like you've decided to do what you feel is best for your life, I'm doing what's best for my life. Let's just go and get it over with."

Sounding defeated, he said, "I'll see you in a little while," and he hung up the telephone.

Even though I knew in my heart that your father was doing the right thing by marrying Yvette, I was hurt because he chose her over me. So, I couldn't give him what he wanted (which was you) because he couldn't give me what I wanted (him). As much as I hate to admit it, I wanted Andre more than I wanted you. It was a messed up situation, and your life hung in the balance because of it.

We were two subdued individuals riding to Englewood that day. We tried to make conversation, but it was a struggle. Thank God for the radio. The silence between us was deafening. In one of our attempts at conversation, Andre said he told his father about my pregnancy and the planned abortion.

"My dad said we're going to go to hell for this," he said.

I didn't reply. I just continued to look out of the car window. I don't know if his father really believed that, or if he was just sounding off because he was disappointed and annoyed with Andre for getting involved with me.

We arrived at the doctor's office on time. I was relieved to see that it didn't look like the same place I had gone to a few years earlier with Donald. For the first time, I wasn't alone when I signed in, took my seat, and waited to have my third abortion. Andre was by my side.

We sat there silently until my name was called. I followed the nurse to an examination room where I was told to undress. Minutes later, I was examined by the physician. When he was done, he began to administer the anesthesia. Before I knew it, I felt my body going limp, and I couldn't keep my eyes open.

When it was over, I was taken to the recovery room. I woke up, still dazed from the anesthesia, and laid there trying to make sense of my life over the past six months. I was appalled by the thought that I had had two abortions within a six-month period. I was utterly ashamed and remorseful. At that moment, I promised God and myself that I would never, ever have another abortion.

The nurse came in to check my vitals and told me I could get dressed. *Thank God*, I thought. I couldn't wait to get out of there. I dressed and went to the nurse's station to get my prescription. When I returned to the waiting room, Andre was right where I left him, looking like he had just lost his best friend. I walked over to him and told him we could leave.

"Are you okay?" he asked.

"Yeah, I'm okay."

He took my hand in his as we walked out of the doctor's office. That small gesture spoke volumes. He always seemed to know what to say or do. I felt safe with him, and I was going to miss that.

The ride back to my house was a quiet one. I was sleepy, and, in all honesty, I didn't feel there was anything else for us to talk about. He was getting married in a few weeks, our baby was gone, and our affair was over. We had definitely come to the end of our road. In a strange way, I felt relieved. I wanted my life to return to the boring yet tranquil existence I had going when your father entered it. What began with two people enjoying stolen moments turned into our own personal soap opera, and I'd had enough of the drama. I was finally ready to let Andre go.

My apartment was nice and quiet when we walked in. Your brothers were spending the weekend with my mom. Stacy was between apartments, and was staying with me for a few days until her new apartment was ready. She was in the kitchen on the telephone when we arrived. We waved hello, and I kept walking to my bedroom. Andre followed me and asked if I needed anything before he left. I told him no and that I was going to take a nap. I undressed and got into my bed while he stood in the doorway watching. He walked over to the bed and sat down. "Andre, I know you have to go home. I'm okay."

Instead of getting up to leave, he laid down next to me and held me in his arms. We stayed that way until I fell asleep. I slept for several hours, and when I awoke, Andre was gone. I reached over to turn the light on and noticed there was a piece of paper lying on the pillow next to me. It was a note from Andre that said:

"Mon amour, I'm so sorry." Andre.

A warm feeling engulfed me as I turned the light off and went back to sleep holding on to that note.

The next day was Sunday, and all I wanted to do was go to church. Stacy was already up and getting dressed. When I saw her, she smiled and said, "I was about to come in there and see if you were still alive."

"Barely," I said.

"Are you going to church?" she asked.

"Just as fast as I can get there," I said.

"You okay, girl?" Stacy asked.

"No, but I'm going to be. This too shall pass."

"It will. Andre was messed up when he left yesterday. I bet if he had his way he'd marry you *and* Yvette."

"What did he say to you?" I asked.

"He said he never wanted to hurt you."

"I know that. Did he tell you he wanted me to have the baby?"

"Yeah, he mentioned that too. He really feels terrible about the abortion."

"I know. So do I. But it's over now, and I'm ready to move on."

Stacy gave me one of her smirks and said, "Yeah, right! All Jelly Butt got to do is call you on the phone and say *let's* and you'll say *go*."

"No, not anymore! I'm serious this time, girl. It's over."

"If you say so."

Stacy walked over and gave me a hug and said, "I'm just messing with you, girl. You're going to be fine."

The End of the Road

I got through the rest of the month of April, and by the time mid-May had arrived, I was feeling a lot better than I had in months. My life was slowly returning to normal. Andre and I were history. We both made a conscious effort to go out of our way to avoid each other. It was necessary if we were to go on with our separate lives. The chemistry between us made it impossible for us to have a platonic relationship. We were like two people on the *Love Boat* going to *Fantasy Island*. The trouble with our fantasy was it threatened to destroy our reality. So we played it safe and didn't see each other if at all possible.

At work one day, one of my co-workers handed me a stack of airline tickets to sort and match with the itinerary printouts. To my surprise, there were two airline tickets in the stack issued to Mr. Andre Walker and Mrs. Yvette Walker. I couldn't believe my eyes! That was the last thing I wanted to see, and the last thing I wanted to know was the actual date of his wedding. Just knowing it was in June was enough information for me. I couldn't believe Andre had the nerve to book his honeymoon flight, hotel, and rental car through the company travel department, knowing I worked there! I sat at my desk dumbfounded.

Sorting the tickets and matching them with the itineraries was a function we rotated in the office. That week just happened to be my week. Once the tickets and the itineraries were put in envelopes, we called clients to inform them that their tickets were ready for pick-up. Well, that was one phone call I wasn't about to make. I gave his tickets to another co-worker and asked her if she'd notify Mr. Walker that his tickets were ready, and I prayed I wouldn't be anywhere in sight when he came for them. God answered my prayers. As it turned out, Andre didn't pick up his tickets until the next morning. I was late to work that day, and as I was approaching my office, I saw him coming out the door, looking at the tickets in his hands. I stopped dead in my tracks and watched him walk away in the opposite direction. He never saw me.

Andre and Yvette were married the following month, in Pennsylvania. For the remainder of my employment at Prudential, I continued to avoid having contact with your father. At times we would bump into each other, but we always kept it brief. Later that year, I left Prudential. During my last day at work, I called Andre and told him I was moving on to a new job. We met in the annex that afternoon.

"Thanks for calling me, Joy," he said.

"I wanted to let you know I was leaving."

"Where's your new job?"

"I'll be working for Seton Hall Law School," I said.

"Even though I don't see you that much anymore, I'm going to miss the possibility of seeing you," he said.

"I'm going to miss the possibility of seeing you too."

We stood there smiling at each other for what seemed like the longest moment. "Joy, I'm here if you ever need me. You know that, don't you?" he asked.

"Yes."

I felt my restraints weakening, so I said good-bye and quickly walked away. That was the last time I saw your father.

Not only did I start a new job, but the following month my children and I moved into my sister's house in Orange, New Jersey. It felt like I was really starting over. I had a new job and a new residence, and no memories of Andre in either place. It was really over. Once my phone number changed, Andre and I lost contact. Stacy and I didn't discuss him either. It was a silent agreement between the two of us that Andre Walker was a topic that was off limits.

I don't know how things turned out for your father. I assume he and Yvette stayed together and probably had other children. I pray his decision to marry Yvette brought him happiness.

December baby, just as I can never forget you, I'll never forget your father. Despite his back being against the wall, if I had relented and agreed to have you, he would have welcomed you with open arms. Perhaps he still would have married Yvette, but I believe he would have tried, with all of his might, to be a positive presence in your life. That is the kind of man he was.

I, on the other hand, was hurt, and I used you to get back at your father. I retaliated by denying him the child he wanted. That was wrong. It was terribly wrong. I allowed my emotions to cause me to act selfishly rather than to allow my love to move me to do what was right. I deeply regret my actions and ask for your forgiveness.

I'm a brand new woman. That silly woman is gone for good. Jesus is Lord of my life, and I have His promise of eternal life in heaven. When I get there, I'm going to find you and lavish my love on you, my darling December baby.

Your loving mother,

Joy

Quiet Moments: Write Your Own Letter

AND IN
Conclusion

I PRESS—
Toward the Mark of the High Call

"Brethren, I count not myself to have apprehended: but this
one thing I do, forgetting those things which are behind, and
reaching forth unto those things which are before,
I press toward the mark for the prize of the high calling
of God in Christ Jesus."
(PHILIPPIANS 3:13, 14)

Writing these letters has served as a catharsis in my healing process. A purging has taken place in my soul and spirit. No longer will the disappointments and regrets of the past keep me bound. I am free to move on and receive the good things God has in store for me, as promised in His Word. I am finally free, and it feels great! I am ready to move into the next phase of my life, without guilt, shame, or self-condemnation.

I realize now that I was looking for love in all the wrong places. When a girl grows up without the love of a father, she longs for male love and acceptance. Those are two basic needs of every human being. In my quest to capture the heart and love of a man, I entered relationships that were doomed from the beginning, for one reason or the other.

I forgive myself for the mistakes I've made, and I forgive Donald, Michael and Andre. I don't know where they are, but I wish them well and pray they are happy. I may not ever see them again in this life, but I can honestly say I am at peace, and I grateful to them for the fond memories, especially those with Andre.

I've learned that people come into your life for a reason or a season. Donald came for a reason, and I believe it was to teach me what love is *not*. His need to control and his willingness to share me with other men did not equate to true love. Donald revealed to me the kind of man I *don't* want in my life.

Michael was for a season. For over twenty-seven years, I allowed Michael to drop in and out of my life. He was a distraction that occurred usually when I was coasting along peacefully. I would be headed in the right direction, and he would detour me left and steer me off my path. By the time he was gone again, I would have to regain my footing and get refocused. My self-esteem suffered in the process, because I was left feeling used. Why did I allow this to happen for such a long period of time? My only answer is that I couldn't resist him. I mistakenly believed the sex was worth it.

Andre was for a reason. He revealed to me the kind of man and love I needed. His sensitivity and passion mirrored mine. He was easy to be with. I was comfortable with him, and most importantly, I genuinely liked him as a person. It's like having your favorite chair to come home to after a hard day at work. When you finally sit down and relax, the world is beautiful again. Because of Andre, I know what I'm looking for in a mate.

How does my story end? I can't say, as it is still unfolding. But I can tell you this. Once I placed my focus on my children and on developing a personal relationship with Jesus, my life changed for the better.

After Andre, I began to take my walk with God seriously. Although I had been in church all my life, I didn't know the importance of cultivating a personal relationship with God through His Son, Jesus. Thank God I found a church where I was able to grow in the knowledge of God—who He is and what His will is for my life— and how to walk with Him on a daily basis.

Singing in the choir was a great release and a source of comfort for me. Those Baptist hymns and gospel songs got me through many lonely nights. Through it all, a strength, which I now know is the strength of God, was forming in me, replacing many of my former weaknesses. I was becoming a happier person, as the peace of God, the love of God, the joy of God, and the wisdom of God, were being formed within me. My children's lives were being impacted by the change that was occurring in me. I was thriving, and so were they. Not only was I getting my act together, but their father, Rodney, was spending quality time with them. Things were finally falling into place.

For the next seven years, I refrained from entering any dead-end relationships. My focus was on marriage and giving my children a solid, Christian home. I dated occasionally, but once it was established that we were going in opposite directions, that was it for me. I knew what I wanted, and I was learning that I didn't have to settle for less than that. I made it a practice not to entertain men in my home. I didn't want my sons exposed to different men. I was possessive where my children were concerned. I had heard horror stories about men coming into a woman's life trying to run her house and children. That was not about to happen to me. If a man wanted to date me, he had to take me out or keep stepping. He wasn't about to sit up in my house, wearing out my furniture and eating up my food.

In the spring of 1986, I met Keith Swanson. He was a kind, Christian, single man who joined my church. He was five years younger than I was, and, needless to say, very handsome. At the time of our meeting, I had been celibate for three years. I believed he was the answer to my prayers. As we slowly got to know each other, we began dating. It wasn't long before we discovered that we were on the same page regarding marriage and family. My children got to know him also, mainly through their contact with him at church. However, once we decided to become a couple, they sometimes joined us on our dates. He was wonderful with the boys, and they liked him a lot.

We were engaged that summer and married the following January. Our relationship wasn't the most passionate, but the love was genuine. The following November I gave birth to my third son. He was Keith's only child, and the apple of his eye. My life was on course, and I had the marriage and home I had dreamed of since I was a little girl. I owe it all to God for transforming me from that silly woman I used to be into a loving wife and mother.

Keith was a good man, and I tried to make it with him. But something was missing. I longed for the passion, intimacy, and coziness I had experienced with Andre. When I tried to initiate intimacy with Keith, he would think I wanted sex. He had no clue that they are two different things. For instance, once we were in our bedroom watching a movie. He was sitting on the floor at the foot of the bed, and I was lying on the bed. I said, "Hey, baby, why don't you come and lie on the bed with me?"

"No, that's okay. I want to sit down here on the floor," he said.

Like a lot of men, he didn't get it. The issue wasn't about him sitting on the floor. It was about us being together as lovers, not just two adults in a room watching a movie. Over time, his emotional detachment became difficult for me to deal with. I wanted so much more from him. We never achieved the level of intimacy and comfort I desired, and after ten years of marriage, we called it quits and went our separate ways.

I am single again, but not alone. I am in a very happy and peaceful place. Life is good. My children are grown, and I have two beautiful grandchildren. I haven't met Mr. Right yet, but I remain hopeful. It happened once, and it can happen again. When it does, maybe I'll write and tell you all about it. Stay tuned!

A Word of Inspiration from Julia

Joy's story isn't unique. There are many women who have found themselves in her shoes and have had to make the same difficult choices. If you have been scarred by the shame and guilt of abortion, I hope you have been inspired to begin the healing process:

1. Seek God's forgiveness
2. Forgive yourself and others
3. Find a way to purge yourself of all negative emotions
4. Forget the past and move forward

If you would like to know Jesus, you can. He's just a prayer away. He'll come into your heart if you invite Him. All you have to do is pray the following prayer:

Jesus, I recognize and admit that I am a sinner. I turn away from my sins and confess with my mouth and believe in my heart that God raised you from the grave, and you are Lord. Thank you for saving me. Amen.

It's that simple. If you prayed that prayer, you are now a part of the body of Christ. Salvation and eternal life are yours! I encourage you to find a Word-based church, so you can learn all that is included in your salvation package, what your rights are as a born-again believer, and how to apply the scriptures to your everyday life. You'll be so glad you did!

About the Author

Julia Stewart Melton is a freelance writer, senior editor, and vocalist. Born and raised in Newark, New Jersey, Julia currently resides in Atlanta, Georgia. She is passionate about the call on her life to inspire and uplift hurting people through her literary works, music, and speaking engagements. Julia is the mother of three sons and a member of World Changers Church International.

Letters

TO MY

Children

DEVOTIONAL

A FEW WORDS OF
encouragement ...

After my abortions, I struggled with grief and self-unforgiveness for a very long time. I had no idea I would grieve the loss of my babies to such a great extent. Likewise, I had no idea that the guilt and shame would haunt me for many years. But, thank God for His Word. It got me through some very dark days (and nights). Through the study of the Word, I learned there is nothing I can't overcome in this life when I seek help, guidance, and wisdom from my heavenly Father.

My 31-day devotional is a compilation of Scriptures I used to overcome my pain, and finally get to the place of forgiveness for myself for what I had done. As a result, I am no longer a victim because of my actions, but an overcomer.

I pray these Scriptures will strengthen and encourage you as much as they have strengthened and encouraged me.

DAY 1

"He heals the brokenhearted
And binds up their wounds"
(Psalm 147:3).

———∽∽———

God loves you with an everlasting love. There is nothing you can do or say that will ever change the way He feels about you. He wants to wrap His loving arms around you and take away your pain. So, open your mind to the truth that He loves you, and allow Him to heal you with His powerful, unconditional love. Receive His love today!

PRAYER

Father, in the name of Jesus, I thank You for your unconditional love. I thank You for healing my broken heart and binding up my wounds. I ask You to give me the strength to no longer dwell on the bad choices I have made. I thank You for the grace to put the past behind me and to move forward with You. In Jesus' name, Amen.

CONFESSION

I declare and decree in the name of Jesus,
that God loves me. He is not mad at me. Therefore,
I am free from the guilt and pain of my past.

DAY 2

"Surely he hath borne our griefs, and carried our sorrows:
yet we did esteem him stricken, smitten of God, and afflicted"
(ISAIAH 53:4).

Stop carrying your grief (sickness, disease, anxiety, and affliction). Jesus bore all of your griefs upon Himself. He has carried away your sorrows.

PRAYER

Father, in the name of Jesus, I thank You that I do not have to
bare my grief. Thank You for carrying them away.
Thank You for giving me the strength to overcome grief
and sorrow. In Jesus' name, Amen.

CONFESSION

I declare and decree in the name of Jesus, that I no longer bare
my grief. Jesus has carried away my grief and sorrow. All pain is
gone, and I have peace in my heart and soul.

DAY 3

"Blessed are they that mourn: for they shall be comforted"
(MATTHEW 5:4).

Loss always causes us to mourn. It could be the loss of a person or an object. Or, it could be the loss of our fellowship with God because of sin. The good news is, when we mourn because of sin, we are blessed because of God's forgiveness—the source of our comfort.

PRAYER

Father, in the name of Jesus, I thank You for blessing me with Your comfort. Because you have forgiven me, I no longer mourn the loss of fellowship with You. Thank You, in Jesus' name. Amen.

CONFESSION

I declare and decree in the name of Jesus, that I am no longer mournful. I am blessed, and comforted. I am in fellowship with God, and all sadness is gone.

DAY 4

"Blessed be God, even the Father of our Lord Jesus Christ, the Father of mercies, and the God of all comfort; Who comforteth us in all our tribulation, that we may be able to comfort them which are in any trouble, by the comfort wherewith we ourselves are comforted of God"
(2 CORINTHIANS 1:3-4).

———

Just as God has been your comfort in hard times, He wants you to comfort someone who is going through hard times. You are blessed to be a blessing. Be there for that person like God was there for you.

PRAYER

Father, in the name of Jesus, thank You for bringing me to someone who is going through hard times. Thank You for showing me how to comfort that person just as You have comforted me. In Jesus' name, Amen.

CONFESSION

I declare and decree in the name of Jesus, that I have the wisdom to bring comfort to someone who is hurting. I am blessed to be a blessing!

DAY 5

"Casting all your care on Him, for He cares for you"
(1 P ETER 5 : 7).

God cares for you so much! He never intended for you to carry your cares because He doesn't want you stressed out, unable to sleep, and full of anxiety. Instead, He wants you to trust Him enough to let Him perfect everything that concerns you. When you cast your cares on Him, you are saying, "Father, I trust You and Your plan for my life."

PRAYER

Father, in the name of Jesus, I thank You that I can cast my cares on You. Because you care for me, I don't have to worry or fret when life gets hard. I can rest knowing that You are perfecting everything that concerns me. Thank You for carrying my burdens. In Jesus' name, Amen.

CONFESSION

I declare and decree in the name of Jesus, that I trust God. I don't worry about anything, because He cares for me. I cast every care on Him. Therefore, when I'm faced with challenges, I don't worry. I remain calm and stress free.

DAY 6

"Yes, my soul, find rest in God; my hope comes from him"
(PSALM 62:5, NIV).

There's nothing like having the faith to leave your cares with God. Your faith should hang on nothing but the promise of God. Make God your only dependence, and never trust in anything else.

PRAYER

Father, in the name of Jesus, I thank You that I can find rest in You. My hope and trust is in You. In Jesus' name, Amen.

CONFESSION

I declare and decree in the name of Jesus, that I place my cares in God's capable hands. I hang on to the promise of God and depend on nothing and no one but Him.

DAY 7

"Come unto me, all ye that labour and are heavy laden, and I will give you rest. Take my yoke upon you, and learn of me; for I am meek and lowly in heart: and ye shall find rest unto your souls. For my yoke is easy, and my burden is light"
(MATTHEW 11:28-30).

When life doesn't always go the way you want it to, guilt, disappointments, and regrets can cause you to feel burdened down and distressed. That's the time to go to God, and His Word. Your soul, which is your mind, will, and emotions will find rest. He wants you to be yoked to Him, not to your burdens. His yoke is easy, and His burden is light.

PRAYER

Father, in the name of Jesus, I thank You that I can come to You when I feel burdened and weighed down. I thank You that as the weight is shifted from my shoulders to Yours, I find rest for my soul. In Jesus' name, Amen.

CONFESSION

I declare and decree in the name of Jesus, that I am yoked to God. I am not weighed down by my situation and circumstances. I find rest in God and His Word.

DAY 8

"Repent ye therefore, and be converted,
that your sins may be blotted out, when the times of
refreshing shall come from the presence of the Lord"
(ACTS 3:19).

The prerequisite of having your sins blotted out is repentance. Once you have repented, you can look forward to God blotting them out forever. Also, repentance ushers in a season of refreshing that will change your life for the better.

PRAYER

Father, in the name of Jesus, I repent of my sins. I thank You for
blotting them out forever. I desire to be in Your presence and
experience times of refreshing. I thank You for Your grace and
mercy toward me. In Jesus' name, Amen.

CONFESSION

I declare and decree in the name of Jesus,
that my sins have been blotted out. I enter a season of
refreshing as I dwell in the presence of the Lord.

DAY 9

*"For as the heaven is high above the earth, so great is his mercy
toward them that fear him. As far as the east is from the west,
so far hath he removed our transgressions from us"*
(PSALM 103:11-12).

God is not holding anything against you. All of your sins have
been removed by a miracle of His great love and mercy. They
have been removed so far that it can never be brought back again.
They are gone! So, let them go. Forget them. God has.

PRAYER

*Father, in the name of Jesus, I thank You for Your mercy and
love. I thank You for removing my sins far, far away from me.
I thank You that they can never be brought back. Because you
don't remember them, I can forget them too. I thank You that
I can move forward knowing that You have forgiven all of my
transgressions. In Jesus' name, Amen.*

CONFESSION

*I declare and decree in the name of Jesus, that I am free!
My past mistakes no longer has me in bondage. I have been
forgiven, my sins have been removed far from me,
and God loves me with an everlasting love.*

DAY 10

"I, even I, am he that blotteth out thy transgressions
for mine own sake, and will not remember thy sins"
(ISAIAH 43:25).

———❧———

As far as God is concerned, you have a clean slate. He does not hold your transgressions against you. And the good news is, He doesn't even remember them! His grace and love for you is greater than any transgression you can, or will, commit. Rejoice in knowing that you are deeply loved by your heavenly Father.

PRAYER

Father, in the name of Jesus, I thank You for Your unconditional love. Because of Your love for me, I am forgiven. Father, I thank You for not holding my transgressions against me. Thank you for giving me a clean slate. In Jesus' name, Amen.

CONFESSION

I declare and decree in the name of Jesus, that I am deeply loved and forgiven by my heavenly Father. My transgressions have been blotted out, and God does not remember them. Therefore, I do not remember them either.

DAY 11

*"Brethren, I count not myself to have apprehended: but this
one thing I do, forgetting those things which are behind, and
reaching forth unto those things which are before, I press toward
the mark for the prize of the high calling of God in Christ Jesus"*
(PHILIPPIANS 3:13-14).

Get rid of wrong attitudes, habits and behaviors from your past.
God wants you to leave the past in the past, and pursue the future.
To do this you must develop and maintain a positive attitude. Your
mind must be willing to seek and achieve the prize of the high
calling of Christ for your life.

PRAYER

*Father, in the name of Jesus, I thank You for the grace to leave
the past in the past. I release myself from the pain and guilt I
have felt for so long. Thank You for helping me to develop a
positive attitude, and to move forward towards You and Christ's
perfection. In Jesus' name, Amen.*

CONFESSION

*I declare and decree in the name of Jesus, that I don't think about
those things that are behind me. They no longer cause me pain,
guilt, and grief. I press toward the mark of the high calling of God!*

DAY 12

*"In my distress I cried unto the L*ORD*, and he heard me"*
(P SALM 120:1).

———∾∾———

David was distressed because of the slander that was effecting his reputation. Sometimes people you have confided in will turn on you and tell your deep, dark secrets to others. In some cases, they exaggerate or even lie about what they know. When that happens, turn the situation over to the Lord. Cry out to Him, and He will hear you.

PRAYER

Father, in the name of Jesus, thank You for hearing me when I cry out to You. I praise You for delivering me from those who set out to hurt me with their words. Thank you for taking away my distress. In Jesus' name, Amen.

CONFESSION

I declare and decree in the name of Jesus, that I am no longer distressed by the slanderous words of others. God has heard my cry! I am delivered, and I have a good reputation.

DAY 13

"I will lift up mine eyes unto the hills,
from whence cometh my help. My help cometh
from the LORD, which made heaven and earth"
(PSALM 121:1-2).

When the walls of your world come crashing in around you, lift up your head and get excited because it is an opportunity for the Creator of heaven and earth to do something marvelous in your life. He is the source of help to everyone who will look to Him.

PRAYER

Father, in the name of Jesus, I thank You for being my help.
Thank You for giving me the grace to endure the pressure. You
are my everything! In Jesus' name, Amen.

CONFESSION

I love the Lord my God with all of my heart, all my soul,
and all my strength, and all of my might.

DAY 14

"The Lord is a shelter for the oppressed,
a refuge in times of trouble"
(PSALM 9:9, NIV)

———◦◦———

Whenever you feel oppressed and burdened down, remember the Lord is your shelter from the storms of life. He will keep you safe and strong when you are feeling weak and powerless.

PRAYER

Father, in the name of Jesus, thank You for being my shelter that I can run to when I'm feeling oppressed and weak. Thank You for keeping me when I am in trouble. In Jesus' name, Amen.

CONFESSION

I declare and decree in the name of Jesus, that God is my refuge in the times of trouble. He keeps me safe from all harm.

DAY 15

"He that believeth on him is not condemned: but he that believeth not is condemned already, because he hath not believed in the name of the only begotten Son of God"
(JOHN 3:18).

———~~———

God is saying that if you believe in His Son, Jesus, you are not judged (or condemned) because of your transgressions. However, those who do not believe in (or reject) His Son, are already condemned. Belief in Jesus as the Son of God is the source of your justification, which frees you from condemnation.

PRAYER

*Father, in the name of Jesus, I thank You for Your Son, Jesus.
I thank You that He is the source of my justification.
I thank You that because of Jesus, I can live free from all guilt and shame. In Jesus' name, Amen.*

CONFESSION

*I declare and decree in the name of Jesus, that I believe in Jesus.
I believe He is the son of God, and the source of my justification.
Therefore, I do not feel condemned by the bad choices I've made in the past. I no longer carry the burden of guilt and shame. I am free!*

DAY 16

"There is therefore now no condemnation to them which are in Christ Jesus, who walk not after the flesh, but after the Spirit" (ROMANS 8:1).

God wants you to know that you are not guilty. You have been found innocent and no sentence is inflicted. By His grace, you will not face the condemnation of God. Also, you must understand that your justification is found in Christ alone—in His finished work on the cross—not in what you do or don't do.

Prayer

Father, in the name of Jesus, I thank You for Your grace.
I thank You that I have been found not guilty.
I ask that You help me to see myself as
You do—innocent of all charges. In Jesus' name, Amen.

Confession

I declare and decree in the name of Jesus,
that I do not face the condemnation of God. Therefore, I do not
condemn myself. I see myself as God sees me. I am innocent!

DAY 17

"The Lord upholdeth all that fall,
and raiseth up all those that be bowed down"
(P s a l m   1 4 5 : 1 4).

Many times, the mistakes and choices you make will cause you to feel as though you are carrying the weight of the world on your shoulders. It is in those times that you can turn to God, Who will raise you up with His love and tender mercy.

Prayer
Father, in the name of Jesus, thank You for raising
me up when I fall. Thank You for Your love and mercy.
I receive them both in the name of Jesus, Amen.

Confession
I declare and decree in the name of Jesus,
that when I fall, God raises me up. His love and mercy
for me keeps me all the days of my life.

DAY 18

"For all have sinned, and come short of the glory of God;"
(ROMANS 3:23)

God does not want you to be self-judgmental. Neither does He want you to hold your actions against yourself. Once you have repented, you are no longer bound by its judgement. You must forgive yourself just as you would forgive another. You must do this so that you will receive His forgiveness and walk in a new level of His grace and mercy.

PRAYER

Father, in the name of Jesus, I thank You that I can repent of my sins and receive Your forgiveness. Thank You for Your grace and mercy. And I thank You for helping me to forgive myself. I let it go now! In Jesus' name, Amen.

CONFESSION

I declare and decree in the name of Jesus,
that I no longer hold my sins against myself.
I have repented, and therefore, I am no longer bound by its judgement. Just as God has forgiven me, I forgive myself.

DAY 19

"If we confess our sins, he is faithful and just to forgive us our sins, and to cleanse us from all unrighteousness"
(1 JOHN 1 : 9).

God is so faithful. When you confess your sins, He won't let you down. He will forgive you, and cleanse you from all wrongdoing. Remember, when Jesus died on the cross He solved the sin problem not only for you, but for the whole world. So, walk in His light knowing that you are forgiven.

PRAYER

Father, in the name of Jesus, I thank You for being so faithful to me. I know that I can boldly confess my sins and receive Your forgiveness. Thank You for cleansing me from all unrighteousness. I thank You for Your love and tender mercies. In Jesus' name, Amen.

CONFESSION

I declare and decree in the name of Jesus, that I am forgiven. I am cleansed from my wrongdoings, and I walk in the light, love, and mercy of God. I walk in the light, love, and mercy of God.

DAY 20

"We are made right with God by placing our
faith in Jesus Christ. And this is true for everyone
who believes, no matter who we are"
(ROMANS 3:22, NLT).

———◦◦◦———

We are made right in God's sight when we trust in Jesus Christ to take away our sins. And we all can be saved in this same way, no matter who we are or what we have done.

PRAYER

Father, in the name of Jesus, thank You for making me righteous
and taking away my sins. I am grateful that because I trust in
Your Son, Jesus, there is nothing I can do that will ever change
my right standing with You. In Jesus' name, Amen.

CONFESSION

I declare and decree in the name of Jesus that in God's sight I am
the righteous. My faith and trust is in Jesus. Therefore, no matter
what I've done, I can never be an outcast.

DAY 21

"And forgive us our sins; for we also forgive every one
that is indebted to us. And lead us not into temptation;
but deliver us from evil"
(L U K E   1 1 : 4).

───────ᔋᕽᔋ───────

Forgiving those who are indebted to us isn't always easy, but it
is necessary. To forgive is a great evidence of grace. When grace
comes into your heart, it sweetens the heart and fills it with love.

PRAYER

Father, in the name of Jesus, because You have forgiven me of
my sins, I can forgive _____.
I release this person to You and Your love. In Jesus' name, Amen.

CONFESSION

I forgive and release others who have wronged,
sinned, and trespassed against me.

DAY 22

"And whenever you stand praying, if you have anything against anyone, forgive him and let it drop (leave it, let it go), in order that your Father Who is in heaven may also forgive you your [own] failings and shortcomings and let them drop" (MARK 11:25, AMP).

It is very important to forgive people who have played a part in your pain and suffering. Don't complain to God about what they did, instead, pray to God about it and forgive them in your heart. Although they may not verbally hear you say, "I forgive you", you will release them from the offense. As a result, your heart is opened to receive God's forgiveness for your transgressions.

PRAYER

Father, in the name of Jesus, I thank You that I am healed from all of my past hurts. Thank You for giving me the strength to forgive those who have hurt me. I release them now, and I let it go! I thank You that my heart is open to receive Your love, mercy and forgiveness. In Jesus' name, Amen.

CONFESSION

I declare and decree in the name of Jesus, that I am healed from the pain of my past. I have a forgiving heart, and I do not hold a grudge against anyone for anything.

DAY 23

*"Judge not, and ye shall not be judged: condemn not, and ye
shall not be condemned: forgive, and ye shall be forgiven:"*
(LUKE 6:37)

Do you want God to judge you without mercy or compassion?
Well, He will use the same standards of judgment to you that you
use toward others. If you are quick to condemn others, He will be
quick to condemn you. Also, if you are unwilling to forgive the
offenses of others, God will be unwilling to forgive your sins.

PRAYER

*Father, in the name of Jesus, I thank You for
Your mercy and compassion. Thank You for helping me
to show the same mercy and compassion to those
who have hurt me. In Jesus' name, Amen.*

CONFESSION

*I declare and decree in the name of Jesus,
that I am merciful and compassionate. I forgive the offenses
of others. I do not judge or condemn them.*

DAY 24

"In Him we have redemption (deliverance and salvation)
through His blood, the remission (forgiveness) of our offenses
(shortcomings and trespasses), in accordance with the
riches and the generosity of His gracious favor"
(EPHESIANS 1:7, AMP).

Because of the sacrifice of Jesus, you are free from all penalties
and punishments resulting from your shortcomings and trespasses.
You are free to start over, and live your life to the fullest without
any regrets.

PRAYER

Father, in the name of Jesus, I thank You for redemption through
the blood of Jesus. I thank You for Your favor. I am no longer
ashamed of my past. I hold my head high knowing that I am
forgiven and accepted by You. In Jesus' name, Amen.

CONFESSION

I declare and decree in the name of Jesus, that I am the redeemed
of the Lord. I have deliverance and salvation through Jesus'
precious blood. I am living my best life today and always because
of the riches and the generosity of God's gracious favor on my life.

DAY 25

"Therefore if any man be in Christ, he is a new creature:
old things are passed away; behold, all things are become new"
(2 CORINTHIANS 5:17).

Your old nature is gone. Your old ways are gone. You have a new nature and new ways of doing things. You are a new creation who is no longer a slave to sin. You are now empowered by and for righteousness. You have the power to make better choices and to live a better, happier life.

PRAYER

Father, in the name of Jesus, I thank You that I am a new creature in Christ. My old nature and old ways are passed away. I thank You that all things are new. In Jesus' name, Amen.

CONFESSION

I declare and decree in the name of Jesus, that I am not the person I used to be. I am a new creation in Christ. I no longer make bad choices. I am empowered by and for righteousness, and I have the power to make right choices.

DAY 26

"And I will restore to you the years that the locust hath eaten, the cankerworm, and the caterpiller, and the palmerworm, my great army which I sent among you. And ye shall eat in plenty, and be satisfied, and praise the name of the LORD your God, that hath dealt wondrously with you: and my people shall never be ashamed"
(JOEL 2:25-26).

Like the people in this scripture, God will restore to you all that has been taken or destroyed by negative situations and circumstances. The effect of these great trials in your life can be viewed as the tested genuineness of your faith. And, as a result, you can praise and honor God Who guarded you and kept you through the hardest times of your life. And He promises that you will never be ashamed!

PRAYER

Father, in the name of Jesus, I thank You for guarding and keeping me through my hard times. Thank You for restoring my faith in You. Thank You for restoring everything I've lost. I give You honor and praise for it all, in Jesus' name. Amen.

CONFESSION

I declare and decree in the name of Jesus, that I am restored! My faith, and everything the years of suffering have taken from me has been restored. I have long-term gain from short-term loss.

DAY 27

"Restore unto me the joy of thy salvation;
and uphold me with thy free spirit"
(Psalm 51:12).

If you have lost your joy, you can have joy again. This is what David was praying for in the scripture. Although God didn't take away the joy of your salvation, He is capable of restoring it. He will not only restore it, but will establish you with His free Spirit. In other words, He will restore your joy and will sustain and keep you from falling so that you won't lose your joy again.

PRAYER

Father, in the name of Jesus, thank You for
restoring my joy. Although I lost the joy You gave me,
You love me enough to give it to me again. I am so grateful
and I give You praise for it in Jesus' name, Amen.

CONFESSION

I declare and decree in the name of Jesus, that I have my joy
again. I am no longer a sad or broken person. I am cheerful!
I feel good about myself, and my life is filled with joy.
I bask in the warm sunshine of God's love.

DAY 28

"For I know the plans I have for you,"
declares the LORD, "plans to prosper you
and not to harm you, plans to give you hope and a future"
(JEREMIAH 29:11, NIV).

While you are going through difficult times, cling to this scripture. God will give you hope in the midst of your struggles. However, more importantly, you have security knowing that He will never abandon you, and your future, hope, and prosperity will be fully realized and will not put you to shame.

PRAYER

Father, in the name of Jesus, I thank You for Your plans to
prosper me, and give me hope, and a future. I thank You that
Your plans are good and will not harm me. I praise You for my
glorious future. In Jesus' name, Amen.

CONFESSION

I declare and decree in the name of Jesus that my
future is secure in God. No matter what I go through in this life,
I place my hope and trust in God's plans for me.

DAY 29

"Come now, let us reason together, says the Lord: though your
sins are like scarlet, they shall be as white as snow; though they
are red like crimson, they shall become like wool"
(ISAIAH 1:18).

King David, a murderer and an adulterer, was fully restored by
God once he repented. The same is true for you. No matter what
you've done, once you repent, God will restore you.

PRAYER
Father, in the name of Jesus, I repent. Thank You for restoration
in every area of my life. In Jesus' name, Amen.

CONFESSION
I declare and decree in the name of Jesus that my sins are
forgiven, and I am fully restored by God.

DAY 30

"Confess your sins to each other and pray for each other so that you may be healed. The earnest prayer of a righteous person has great power and produces wonderful results"

(JAMES 5:16, NLT).

———∿∿———

Find someone in your life to confide in so that person can help you, and pray for you to overcome your transgressions. Likewise, if you notice someone struggling with a problem get on your knees and ask God to come to his or her aid. The prayers of a righteous person releases tremendous power and changes everything.

PRAYER

Father, in the name of Jesus, I thank You for surrounding me with righteous people who know the power of prayer. I thank You that as a result of their prayers, I am healed. Thank You for leading me to people that I can help in their time of need. In Jesus' name, Amen.

CONFESSION

I declare and decree in the name of Jesus that I will not point out someone else's flaws. Instead, I will pray for the individual. My prayers are powerful and yield wonderful results.

DAY 31

"I love the LORD, because he hath heard my voice and my
supplications. Because he hath inclined his ear unto me,
therefore will I call upon him as long as I live"
(P S A L M   1 1 6 : 1 - 2) .

You have a Comforter (the Holy Spirit) who gives peace and healing to your hurting heart. Whatever you go through in life, remember you have someone to turn to who hears your prayers. You can rest in the strength of the Holy Spirit, and have comfort that is unspeakable in your darkest hours.

PRAYER

Father, in the name of Jesus, I thank You for hearing
my voice and my supplications. Thank You for Your Holy Spirit
who has restored my peace and healed my hurting heart.
In Jesus' name, Amen.

CONFESSION

I declare and decree in the name of Jesus that
I abide in the peace of God, and I allow His peace to
rule my heart each and every day.